NORTH BRITISH
STEAM LOCOMOTIVES
built 1833-1948
for railways
in Britain

D1556198

NORTH BRITISH

CANVE

Queen's Park Works L? 248.

TEAM LOCOMOTIVES

built 1833–1948 for railways in Britain

JOHN H. COURT

LONDON, TILBURY & SOUTHEND RAILWAY—1908. From 1880, when the L.T.S.R. bought its first locomotive, the railway was essentially a tank engine line and only two 0-6-0 tender engines, bought in 1898, broke the long succession of 4-4-2 and 0-6-2 tanks, which continued until 1912. Of the 0-6-2 variety, only ten were purchased—six in 1903 and four in 1908 and all came from N B L; "Canvey Island" (illustrated) was one of the second batch. Designed by T. Whitelegg, they were essentially for goods traffic; cylinders were 18″ × 26″ and coupled wheels 5′ 3″ diameter. It is interesting to note that the railway's first twelve 4-4-2 tanks came from Sharp, Stewart & Co. in 1880. The first of their type to be built in Britain, they were Sharp's answer to the main line tank problem. So effective were they that they became the "universal" engines of the L.T.S.R. When T. Whitelegg retired his son, R. H. Whitelegg, succeeded him and in 1912 introduced 4-6-4 Baltic tanks—the first in Britain. The N B L 0-6-2s survived for 50 years or more but the Baltics, which never carried L.T.S.R. numbers or livery, had all been scrapped by 1934. The end of the "Tilbury" came in 1912 with its absorption by the Midland Railway. Under grouping it became part of the London, Midland & Scottish Railway; nationalisation took it into the London Midland region but it was later transferred to the Eastern Region of British Railways.

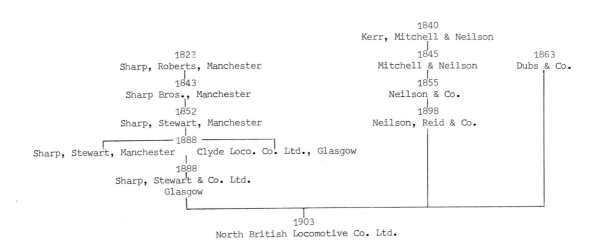

© *copyright D. Bradford Barton*   IRRC   38782D   *ISBN 0 85153 339 6*

printed in Great Britain by H. E. Warne Ltd, London and St. Austell

for the publishers

D. BRADFORD BARTON LTD · Trethellan House · Truro · Cornwall · England

Of the locomotive builders of Britain who were in business from about the 1850s or earlier, the pattern of orders is generally the same. Most started by supplying locomotives for the home railways but within a few years they turned their attention to the building of locomotives for the rapidly proliferating railways of Europe. This was a natural process, since as the number of builders increased, so competition became fiercer and if a company was to stay in the race it had to do more than hold its place; expansion was a policy dictated by circumstances. Furthermore, it was obvious that the home market would diminish as railways became capable of designing and building their own locomotives. The same pattern of events affected the European market—as the major railways become self-sufficient so the volume of orders for builders in Britain shrank. The railways of the world beyond, in Asia, Australia, Africa and North and South America, were to be the big buyers of locomotives and remained so until the last days of steam.

In pre-grouping days, prior to 1923, the larger railways had their own locomotive works while the smaller independent lines still continued to buy from outside builders. With grouping, the "Big Four" (Great Western, London Midland & Scottish, London & North Eastern and Southern railways) concentrated building on their own works but on the occasions when these were, for any reason, overloaded, then orders were placed outside. Nationalisation drastically reduced the work for the independent builders and with dieselisation the steam locomotive for the home railways died a natural death.

In the history of N B L there is a remarkable variety of locomotives built for home railways, more so than most other companies could show. This resulted from the fact that when N B L came into being in 1903 it inherited the history of three famous firms of locomotive builders, the oldest dating back to 1833. These firms were Sharp, Stewart & Co., Neilson, Reid & Co. and Dübs & Co. The several changes of name of two of these three constituent companies makes repetition rather tedious and the family tree (opposite) simplifies the problem. Sharp, Roberts & Co. built their first locomotive in 1833, Neilson & Co. in 1843 and Dübs & Co. in 1865.

Some of the personalities to be found in the N B L story are deserving of something more than a passing reference. First and foremost is the name of Richard Roberts, the man who, by joining Sharp Brothers to form the Sharp, Roberts partnership, designed and built in 1833

the locomotive "Experiment" and, by so doing, opened the first page of N B L history.

Roberts, already in business as an engineer on his own account in Manchester, was, in 1824, approached by a Mr. Ashton and two leading spinners concerning the virtual automation of the spinning mule. His reply was a categoric refusal and to a second approach his reaction was the same. Eventually an appeal was made to one of the Sharp family who, in turn, himself approached Roberts on the subject. By this time Roberts, who had been mulling the idea over, said that he thought he could do the work. Before the end of 1825 he had produced and patented his self-acting spinning mule. In 1828 Roberts was taken into partnership and Sharp, Roberts & Co. came into being. In 1832 he turned his mind to locomotives and work was started on the design for "Experiment". As a one-time man of Maudslay's, Roberts liked and expected to see fine workmanship and his skill and instinctive knowledge of the rightness of things made his later locomotives better than their north country counterparts. The year 1838 saw the arrival of the renowned "Atlas" Class of 2-2-2s with sandwich frames.

Thomas Sharp died in 1842 and in 1843 Roberts retired from the partnership; he died in 1864 and was buried in Kensal Green Cemetery. It is rightly claimed that "the name of Richard Roberts stands for that of the greatest mechanical inventor of the nineteenth century" and the celebrated name of Sharp, Stewart & Co. is but one of the legacies of his genius. At the time of his death he had about 30 patents in his name in England. During his years in the Sharp, Roberts partnership his able assistant and disciple was Charles Beyer who was later to found the famous Manchester firm of Beyer, Peacock & Co. Ltd.

In the story of Neilson, Reid & Co. the figure of Walter Montgomerie Neilson (1819-1889) looms large. The son of an eminent engineer, James Beaumont Neilson (1792-1865), inventor of the bats-wing gas burner, of various improvements in gas manufacture and of the hot blast system of iron manufacture which transformed the Scottish iron industry, he also had an uncle, John Neilson, who was in business as an engineer in Glasgow. With this background it is not surprising to find Walter Neilson already in business in 1840 in a partnership titled Kerr Mitchell & Neilson; his first locomotive, an 0-4-0 for the Glasgow & Garnkirk Railway, was built about 1843. By 1855 the name Neilson & Co. appeared. In 1858 Henry Dübs became works manager and in 1862 he was already a partner and was responsible for the transfer of the works from Hyde Park Street to the new works at Springburn. Dübs resigned in 1863 in order to form the Glasgow Locomotive Works in Polmadie on the South side of the Clyde.

In 1852 James Reid (1823–1894) had joined Neilson as manager of the Hyde Park Street works, a position he retained until 1858 when he left to take up a similar position with Sharp, Stewart & Co. in Manchester. On the resignation of Dübs in 1863, Neilson invited Reid to return as managing partner.

After a violent quarrel with Reid, Neilson withdrew from active management of the Hyde Park works and in 1876 he retired. Reid remained as sole partner until 1893 when he brought in as partners four of his sons, Hugh, John, Andrew and Walter.

When Neilson retired from his own company in 1876 he was not idle for long. By 1884 he had established the Clyde Locomotive Co. Ltd. with works in Springburn and separated only from the works of Neilson, Reid & Co. by the tracks of the North British Railway. In Manchester the Atlas Works of Sharp, Stewart & Co. were becoming an increasing problem because of the lack of rail connection and in 1888 the Clyde Locomotive Co. was acquired and Sharp, Stewart & Co., Atlas Works, Glasgow, was established.

Henry Dübs (1816–1876) came from Guntersblum in Germany and after some experience in engineering in France, came to Britain in 1839 and entered the drawing office of Sharp, Roberts & Co. in Manchester. In 1842 he was Manager at Charles Tayleur's works, in 1857 he moved on to Beyer, Peacock & Co. and 1858 found him in Glasgow with Neilson & Co. At the time of his resignation in 1863 he proceeded to found his own company, Dübs & Co., and in 1865 his Glasgow Locomotive Works (renamed Queens Park Works in 1903) completed its first locomotive, an 0-4-2 with four-wheeled tender, one of ten for the Caledonian Railway.

At the time of the 1903 amalgamation and the formation of N B L the three works—Hyde Park (ex Neilson), Atlas (ex Sharp, Stewart) and Queens Park (ex Dübs)—constituted a total ground area of approximately 60 acres. Prior to 1903 the three firms had built no less than 16,000 locomotives and this figure alone is indicative of the wealth of experience and expertise which became available to N B L.

The locomotive building industry as a whole had seen the end of the boom in the development of the pioneer railways and the settling down was a period of vigorous competition. So, when Mr. Hugh Reid, senior partner in Neilson, Reid & Co., proposed a merger between his company, Sharp, Stewart & Co. and Dübs & Co., it did not take long for matters to be resolved. At the amalgamation the Chairman of the Board was Mr. (later Sir) William Lorimer and the Deputy Chairman and Chief Managing Director Mr. (later Sir) Hugh Reid.

William Lorimer (1844–1922), LL.D., joined Dübs & Co. in 1864, was appointed principal assistant to Mr. Dübs in 1867, became a partner in 1875 and managing partner after the death of Henry Dübs. For 19 years he guided the destinies of N B L through years of peace and war with unswerving loyalty and exceptional ability. His business acumen was one of the Company's greatest assets and in 1920 he was knighted for his services.

Hugh Reid, C.B.E., LL.D., took over the direction of Neilson, Reid & Co. when his father, James Reid, died, and was instrumental in bringing about the 1903 merger which created the largest locomotive building complex in Europe. He was a man of great energy—energy born of an enthusiasm for the task in hand—and the driving spirit of the company. For his services to the industry and to the nation he was awarded a baronetcy.

A large new Administrative Building was opened in 1909 and although this brought the three separate administrative and drawing office staffs together, certain sections retained their identity until organisational stability warranted total integration. By this means friction was avoided and continuity of effort ensured.

It is from the pre-amalgamation records and after that the photographs reproduced in this volume are taken. Selection was not an easy task and, since no two people can ever agree on this matter, some criticism and some disappointments are inevitable. As the illustrations appearing on pages 8, 9 and 11 are not works photographs some explanation concerning them is necessary. The illustration on page 8 is a reproduction of a drawing of Sharp, Roberts' first locomotive, a 2-2-0 built in 1833 and sold to the Liverpool & Manchester Railway. The drawing, done in 1834 by Thomas Turner (a fitter in the employ of the Company), is the only authentic record of this early essay in locomotive design. Named "Experiment", it was not a success but embodied features which are indicative of the designer's ingenuity. The vertical cylinders operated bell-crank levers (via a crosshead and side links) which powered the driving wheels through short connecting rods. The valves, of piston type with internal admission, were operated through parallel motion. After some deliberation the L.M.R. purchased it for £500 but its consumption of coke was excessive. In 1838 it was sold out of railway service.

The illustrations on pages 9 and 11 are from photographs taken about 1860. That of the G.S.W.R.(I) 2-2-2 of 1845 shows the locomotive in its as-built condition while the Neilson 2-2-2 built for the Edinburgh & Glasgow

Railway in 1850 is depicted in its rebuilt condition of 1868, when in North British Railway ownership. The original E.G.R. locomotive of 1850, then named "Wee Scotland", is clearly discernible. The illustration on page 11 of the Cork, Blackrock & Passage Railway's 0-4-2 tank of 1850 is also reproduced from a photograph taken about 1860.

The products of N B L amply illustrate the development of the steam locomotive for the home railways—from "Experiment" of 1833 through the Atlantic era and into the halcyon days of the 4-6-0 and the Pacific. Under grouping the number of orders N B L received diminished considerably and under nationalisation the cut-back was even more severe until, with the acceptance by B.R. of total dieselisation, the steam locomotive faded ignominiously from the railway scene.

Among the locomotives built for the home market there was not the wide variety of types as were shipped overseas. Special designs such as the Fairlie, Mallet, Fell, Abt, Garratt and Modified Fairlie which proliferated beyond the continent of Europe were seldom, if ever, seen in Britain. On the other hand, the requirements and limitations imposed upon locomotive builders in this country did lead to that refinement in design which gave to our railways a long succession of famous locomotives and to our builders the knowledge which enabled them to meet any motive power requirements in the world.

Sharp, Roberts popularised the 2-2-2 wheel arrangement and the renowned "Sharp Singles" were virtually standard products from 1837 to 1857. As a point of interest it was a Sharp 2-2-2, "Odin", which opened the Danish Railways in 1846. From the 2-2-2 the natural progression was to the 4-2-2 with the bogie replacing the leading pair of wheels. A good example is the Neilson-built engine No.123 of the Caledonian Railway (see page 41). The four-coupled engine appeared in 1840, when an 0-4-2 was built for the Taff Vale Railway. As in the case of the "singles", the 2-4-0 was soon to give place to the 4-4-0, a wheel arrangement which was to become one of the most popular in the U.K. In 1844 the six-coupled engine, an 0-6-0 for the Manchester & Birmingham Railway, came from Sharp's Manchester works, followed by variants such as the 2-6-0 and 4-6-0. The first U.K. 2-6-0 or Mogul came from Neilson in 1878 (see page 35). So the progression goes on through the six-coupled and its important variants, the 4-6-0 and 4-6-2.

Railway loading gauge limits in Britain may have been adequate in the early days but as more power and more speed were demanded by the railway operators, those same limits must have appeared to be restrictive. In fact, they forced designers to approach their task with a wary eye on the limitations of size and this, in turn, enforced the constant improvement of standards of thermal and mechanical efficiency. To see how well they succeeded it is only necessary to look at Stephenson's "Rocket" of 1825 and Sir Nigel Gresley's renowned Pacific "Mallard" with its unbeaten world record of 126 m.p.h. for a reciprocating steam locomotive. The British express passenger engine has commanded world-wide admiration, not just because of its performance but for its sheer compactness and clean external appearance. This success was attributable to many sources, not the least of these being the drawing office of N B L, which added much to that perfection of design which typified the great days of steam.

Superheating, when first introduced, did not make very rapid progress and it was not until 1902 that N B L opened a special register for "Superheated Engines". The first locomotives from the N B L works to be so fitted were two for the Cape Government Railways in 1902, while the first U.K. engines were in a batch of 10 for the North Eastern Railway in 1910. While the popularity of the Schmidt superheater is obvious in the early years, the Robinson type first appears in 1912 for a batch of 50 engines for the Great Central Railway and from that point gradually increases in favour. The Phoenix superheater appears in the register for the first and only time in 1912 for four engines for the Furness Railway and the Gresley type, again for the first and only time, appears in 1920 for a batch of 50 engines for the Great Northern Railway. The M & L superheater is first recorded in 1921. The record book ceased to be used in February, 1925, by which time 2,907 engines had been so equipped.

Outside the workshops of British Rail the locomotive industry of Britain has virtually disappeared and with this major industrial eclipse many famous names have merged into the pages of history. Among the many preserved locomotives are some examples of N B L products; some are still in service on railways overseas but, even there, their numbers are diminishing. With the voluntary liquidation of N B L a great company has gone but its name lives on wherever there are railways and whenever the sight or sound or the memory of steam stirs the imagination of men.

All dates in the caption headings are those of the receipt of order by the companies concerned, and do not necessarily agree with the date of delivery. Furthermore, the names of railways and countries are as at the date of the placing of an order. Closures, grouping and subsequent nationalisation have effected radical changes. Rail gauges, other than 4' 8¼", are shown in brackets after the title of the railway. Railways in Ireland are indicated by the suffix (I) following the railway title and preceding the gauge (if any).

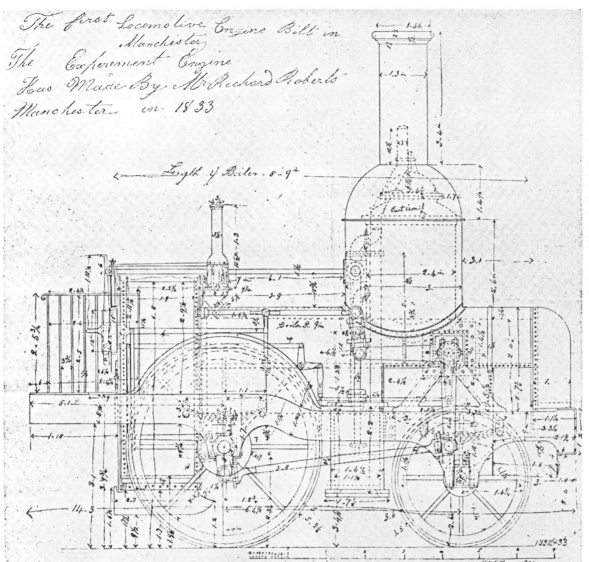

The first Locomotive Engine Built in Manchester,
The Experiment Engine
Has Made By Mr Richard Roberts
Manchester in 1833

Length of Boiler 8'9"

GREAT SOUTHERN & WESTERN RAILWAY (I) [5' 3"]—1845. This illustration of the Sharp-built 2-2-2 is from a photograph taken some years after the locomotive's entry into service—probabl about 1860. One of a batch of nine, it is believed to be depicted in the as-built condition.

LIVERPOOL & MANCHESTER RAILWAY—1833. The drawing reproduced is of the first locomotive in the history of N B L. Built by Sharp, Roberts, the 2-2-0 named "Experiment" was at best an engineering freak and after some reluctance on the part of the L.M.R. it was eventually bought for £500. It was not a success and displayed an excessive appetite for coke, apart from other defects. It entered railway service in 1834 and was disposed of in 1838 (see the Introduction for further details).

EDINBURGH & GLASGOW RAILWAY—1850. The locomotive illustrated was originally bu by Neilson as a 2-2-2 called "Wee Scotland". The E.G.R. was absorbed by the North British Railway 1865 and "Wee Scotland" was rebuilt in 1868 as an inspection or cab engine, being reboilered and saloon added over the rear axle. The illustration depicts the locomotive as rebuilt. It was withdrawn 1906.

CORK, BLACKROCK & PASSAGE RAILWAY (I) [5′ 3″]—1850.   The Cork-Passage section of C.B.P.R. opened in 1850 and locomotive No.1, an 0-4-2 tank built by Sharp, was the first engine to work on it. The photograph reproduced was probably taken in the early 1860s and depicts the locomotive in its as-built condition, with the exception of the cab which was added by the C.B.P.R. some time after 1850.

ST. HELENS RAILWAY—1858. This illustration of the Sharp-built 0-6-0 "Shannon" is believed to be the earliest works photograph of a locomotive built for the home market by one of the constituent companies of N B L. The S.H.R.'s Widnes/Garston section was authorised in 1846 and Widnes/Warrington in 1847; Widnes/Garston was opened in 1852. The line depended for its existence on freight traffic and was promoted by the St. Helens Canal Co. In 1867 it was absorbed by the London & North Western Railway.

LONDON, CHATHAM & DOVER RAILWAY—1861. The 2-4-0 illustrated was one of five delivered by Sharp to the L.C.D.R., a railway which favoured the six-wheel tank engine with a rigid wheel base and the 2-4-0 type in particular. The double frame variety was popular at the time but soon gave place to the inside frame design. The 2-4-0 type illustrated replaced some curious 4-4-0 Crampton locomotives.

OSWESTRY & NEWTOWN RAILWAY—1861. The O.N.R. opened throughout in 1863 and at this time Sharp, Stewart supplied the 0-6-0 locomotive "Cambria" (illustrated), together with three sister engines named "Tubal Cain", "Sir Watkin" and "Cyfronydd". The class became known as the "Queens", after the first 0-6-0 of that name. Coupled wheels were 4' 6" dia. and cylinders 16" × 24". The 1864 amalgamation of the O.N.R. with the Llanidloes & Newtown, Newtown & Machynlleth and the Oswestry, Ellesmere & Whitchurch railways created the Cambrian Railways.

SCOTTISH CENTRAL RAILWAY—1862. Neilson built six 2-4-0 locomotives as illustrated, while others of the same design came from Fairburn and Sharp, Stewart. They followed closely Benjamin Connor's design of 2-4-0 main line goods engines of the Caledonian Railway which were built from 1858 to 1864 and had, like the S.C.R. 2-4-0s, outside bearings for the leading axle. The S.C.R. was taken over by the C.R. in 1865.

AT EASTERN RAILWAY—1863.   For the working of local trains in the London and country
the G.E.R. ordered 20 of the type of 2-4-2 tank locomotive illustrated from Neilson. Robert
ir, the designer, invariably used outside cylinders, in this case 15″ × 22″, while the leading axle was
d in a Bissell truck and the rear axle was rigid. The fixed wheelbase was 12′ and weight in working
37 tons 15 cwt including 500 gallons of water and 50 cu. ft. of fuel.

NORTH STAFFORDSHIRE RAILWAY—1864.   The first section of the N.S.R. (Stoke-Norton Bridge)
opened to both passengers and goods in 1848. In 1864 Neilson built six 0-6-0 locomotives similar to that illustrated.
All entered service in 1865 and were numbered 75 to 80. In 1870 they were re-numbered 84 to 89 and the last
mentioned was in service until 1913.

CON & MERTHYR RAILWAY—1864.   This Sharp-designed 0-6-0 tank was one of seven
ied to the B.M.R. For their day they were considered to be powerful engines and had to work over
with long banks of 1 in 38 to 1 in 40. The long saddle tank carried 1,100 gallons of water; cylinders
17″ × 24″, coupled wheels 4′ 6″ dia. and weight in working order 38 tons.

15

ALEDONIAN RAILWAY—1864. This illustration of C.R. 2-4-0 No.214 poses a curious prob-
m. Examination of the original Neilson photograph shows that it was almost certainly taken when
o.214 was in service and a touched-out Neilson works number plate on the dome is still faintly
scernible; the Caledonian works number (on the frame between the two coupled wheels) has also
·en partly obliterated. Why this hiding of the source of origin?

MANCHESTER, SHEFFIELD & LINCOLNSHIRE RAILWAY—1865. An amalgamation of six companies
operating in the Manchester, Sheffield, Grimsby and Lincolnshire areas in 1849 constituted the M.S.L.R. In 1887
moves were afoot to vest the railway in the Great Northern and Midland railways but negotiations proved
abortive. The 0-6-0 tender engine illustrated was one of 20 built by Sharp, Stewart. In 1897 the railway lost its
identity on its incorporation in the Great Central Railway.

ESS RAILWAY—1865. The F.R. dated back to 1846, when the Barrow to Dalton and Kirkby
opened. Its independence of 58 years came to an end in 1923 when it became part of the London,
d & Scottish Railway. Of the 2-2-2 illustrated, Sharp built four examples. They followed closely
-2 Sharp Standard engine, of which about 600 were built between 1837 and 1857.

SCOTTISH NORTH EASTERN RAILWAY—1864. The S.N.E.R. was one of the many small railways which, when brought into the orbit of the major companies, helped to give Scotland a network of rail access which was remarkably complete. The S.N.E.R. was absorbed by the Caledonian Railway in 1866 and the Neilson-built 0-4-2 No.58 (illustrated) was one of the last engines to be built for the S.N.E.R.

GREAT EASTERN RAILWAY—1867. Neilson built five 2-4-0 tender locomotives similar to the one illustrated. Designed by S. W. Johnson, they were very successful little passenger engines. The "cut" of the cab is reminiscent of Johnson's latter designs of locomotives for the Midland Railway.

...ASGOW & SOUTH WESTERN RAILWAY—1867. The G.S.W.R. was completed in 1850, ...ng through running Gretna/Glasgow via Cumnock. The inside cylinder 2-2-2 tank locomotive ...159 (illustrated) was built by Neilson against a one-off order. The 15″ × 20″ cylinders powered ...le drivers 6′ 0½″ dia. The rear well tank had a capacity of 700 gallons. Weight in working order was ...ons 10 cwt.

MIDLAND RAILWAY—1869.   The order embracing No.724 (illustrated) included 20 of these 0-6-0 double-frame goods locomotives to the design of M. Kirtley. With double solid plate frames, 17″ × 24″ cylinders and 5′ 2½″ diameter coupled wheels they were powerful and long-lived engines.

MIDLAND RAILWAY—1869.   Kirtley's "800" Class 2-4-0s were prominent among the locomotives of their day. The Class numbered 48, Neilson having built 30 of them. Given larger cylinders and boilers they were used for the heaviest express services between London and Carlisle.

MIDLAND RAILWAY—1871.   The "890" Class 2-4-0s were the first M.R. express locomotives to be fitted with cabs. Twenty were built by Neilson. With the introduction of Pullman cars in 1874 the "890s" regularly worked the St. Pancras-Leeds Pullman trains.

CALEDONIAN RAILWAY—1871.   Designed for secondary main line work, six Neilson-built "30" Class 2-4-0 locomotives came out in 1872. Cylinders were 17″ × 24″ and coupled wheels 7′ 2″ dia. The series was rebuilt by McIntosh with an increased heating surface.

MIDLAND GREAT WESTERN RAILWAY (I) [5' 3"]—1871. Of the type of 0-4-0 locomotive illustrated, Neilson built six, including "Dunsandle". Cylinders were 17" × 24", coupled wheels 5' 2" dia. and weight in working order (excluding the 1,600-gallon six-wheeled tender) 31 tons 11 cwt.

GREAT EASTERN RAILWAY—1872. No.168 and four sister 0-4-4 tank engines came from the Neilson works. Cylinders were 17" × 24", coupled wheels 5' 3" dia., tank capacity 970 gallons and fuel space 64 cu. ft. Weight in working order was 44 tons. The coupled wheels were hand braked.

LONDON, CHATHAM & DOVER RAILWAY—1872. The L.C.D.R. was a consistent user of tank engines and Neilson built six of these 0-4-2 back tanks. Cylinders were 17″ × 24″, coupled wheels 5′ 7″ dia., tank capacity 1,110 gallons and fuel space 30 cu. ft.

DUBLIN, WICKLOW & WEXFORD RAILWAY (I) [5′ 3″]—1872. Neilson provided the D.W.W.R. with two of these nicely proportioned 2-2-2 back tank engines. Tank capacity was 550 gallons and fuel space 42 cu. ft. The D.W.W.R. was renamed the Dublin & South Eastern Railway early in 1907.

GREAT NORTHERN RAILWAY—1875. Sharp, Stewart built ten mixed traffic engines of the type illustrated. Designed by Patrick Stirling, these 0-4-2 tender engines had 17½″ × 24″ cylinders and coupled wheels 5′ 7″ dia.

NORTH EASTERN RAILWAY—1873. Fletcher's "901" Class 2-4-0s were very successful engines and worked all the East Coast Scotch express trains. The Class numbered 55 engines, of which Neilson built 10.

NORTH EASTERN RAILWAY—1873. These N.E.R. 0-4-4 back tanks formed a numerous class, to which Neilson added a dozen engines. Cylinders were 16″ × 22″ and coupled wheels 5′ 0″ dia. Tank capacity was 960 gallons, fuel space 84 cu. ft. and weight in working order 44 tons 9 cwt.

CORNWALL MINERALS RAILWAY—1873. The C.M.R. was incorporated in 1873 and absorbed by the Great Western Railway in 1896. The 0-6-0 side tank engines were designed by F. Trevithick for back-to-back working—an early essay in articulation. "Treffrey" (illustrated) was one of 18 (nine pairs) built by Sharp, Stewart.

HIGHLAND RAILWAY—1873. The 4-4-0 "Duke" Class, designed by David Jones, numbered 25 in all, the first ten (or "Bruce" series) coming from Dübs' works. There was a "Lochgorm" and a "Clyde Bogie" series and the three differed in minor details. The "Dukes" derived from the old 2-4-0 "Crewe" type, one of which Jones converted by replacing the leading axle with a bogie. These main line passenger engines were a great success and were the standard for the H.R. for over 20 years.

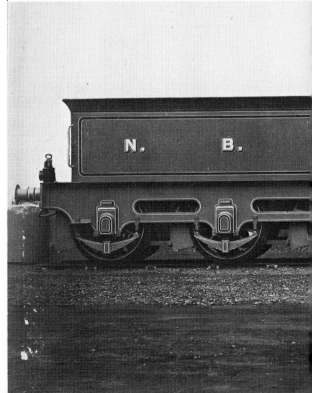

26

NORTH BRITISH RAILWAY—1876. "Abbotsford" and three other 4-4-0s were built by Neilson to Dugald Drummond's design. They were notable examples of the four-coupled bogie type of locomotive. Cylinders were 18″ × 26″, coupled and bogie wheels 6′ 6″ and 3′ 6″ dia. respectively. Total heating surface was 1,099 sq. ft. and weight of the locomotive only in working order 44 tons—14 tons of this being carried on the bogie. A 9′-long coupling rod was something rather unusual in its day.

MIDLAND RAILWAY—1876. S. W. Johnson produced what are considered to be some of the handsomest locomotives built in Britain and this example of his inside cylinder 4-4-0 is a fair sample. Twenty were built by Dübs and were standard on the M.R. for many years. Cylinders were 18″ × 26″, coupled wheels 7′ dia., working pressure 140 lb/sq. in. and weight in working order (engine only) 42 tons 1½ cwt.

LONDON CHATHAM & DOVER RAILWAY—1876. The locomotive illustrated was designed by Kirtley and is another example of the ever popular 4-4-0 wheel arrangement which produced such a wide variety of good looking engines. Six of these L.C.D.R. examples were built by Neilson. Cylinders were 17½″ × 26″, coupled wheels 6′ 6″ dia., total heating surface 1,069 sq. ft., weight in working order (engine only) 42 tons 16 cwt. Tender capacity was 2,550 gallons of water and 190 cu. ft. of coke.

WEST LANCASHIRE RAILWAY—1877.   The 0-4-2 tender locomotive "Edward Holden" (illustrated) was one of six built by Sharp, Stewart. When the company was absorbed by the Lancashire & Yorkshire Railway the W.L.R. had only ten engines. Six were taken over in 1897 by the L.Y.R., but no 0-4-2s were included.

CAMBRIAN RAILWAYS—1877.   "Beaconsfield" and "Hartington" were the first 4-4-0s to grace the metals of the C.R. Built by Sharp, Stewart, they were both powerful and handsome. Cylinders were 17″ × 24″, coupled wheels 5′ 6½″ dia. and weight in working order (engine only) 33 tons 3 cwt.

SOMERSET & DORSET Jnt. RAILWAY—1877. The Johnson 0-6-0 goods locomotive illustrated was designed specially for the S.D.J.R. Numbers 33 to 38 came from Neilson. Cylinders were 17″ × 24″, wheels 4′ 6″ dia., total heating surface 1,104 sq. ft. and weight in working order 30 tons 13 cwt.

GREAT EASTERN RAILWAY—1878.   While these 4–2–2s never earned the reputation of Stirling's 8 ft singles of the Great Northern Railway, they acquitted themselves well. Designed by Massey Bromley, they possessed many individual features, including slide valves which were on top of the 18″ × 24″ cylinders and actuated by rocking shafts. These engines could lift a heavy train out of Liverpool St. and up the Bethnal Green bank without slipping.

MANX NORTHERN RAILWAY [3′ 0″]—1879.   Sharp, Stewart built locomotives Nos.1 and 2 for the M.N.R. T
Isle of Man Railway, from Douglas to Peel, had opened in 1873 but shortage of funds prevented the onward extension
16½ miles to Ramsey. The townspeople promoted the M.N.R. to link their town with the I.O.M.R. at St. John's and
line opened in 1879. Engine details were: cylinders 11″ × 18″; coupled wheels 3′ 9″ dia.; working pressure 130 lb/sq.
tank capacity 400 gallons; weight in working order 17 tons 15 cwt.

GREAT NORTH OF SCOTLAND RAILWAY—1878.   The first section of the G.N.S.R. (Kittybrewster-Huntley)
opened in 1854 and the extension to Keith in 1856. The G.N.S.R. used the outside-cylinder 4-4-0 locomotive for all kinds
of traffic for many years; they formed the backbone of its locomotive stock. No.1 (illustrated) was one of a batch of three
built by Neilson and is a typical example; it was a direct descendant of D. J. Clark's engine of 1861. Note the raised
firebox, the large dome above it and the slotted splasher over the 6′ 1″ drivers. Cylinders were 17½″ × 26″, total heating
surface 1,107 sq. ft. and weight in working order (excluding the 1,950 gallon tender) 39 tons 10 cwt.

MARYPORT & CARLISLE RAILWAY—1881.   The 0-4-0 mineral tank engine illustrated was built by Ne
against a one-off order. Cylinders were 14″ × 20″, wheels 3′ 8″ dia. and weight in working order 26 tons 4 cwt.
M.C.R. was only 28 miles long and opened from Maryport to Aspatria in 1840 and to Carlisle in 1843. The M.
acquired an unique reputation when, on the 17th March, 1849, its Carlisle Crown Street Station—including coal d
station building, track and platforms—was demolished in a night. This resulted from feuding between the M.C.R.
the Lancaster & Carlisle Railway—and on this occasion the latter won!

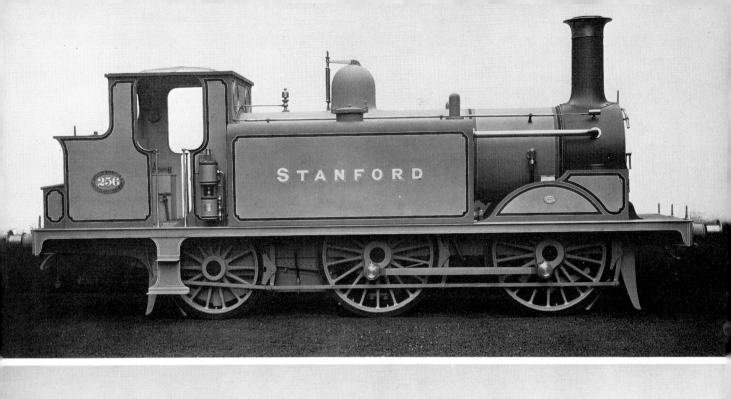

LONDON, BRIGHTON & SOUTH COAST RAILWAY—1882.   No less than 125 of Stroudley's "D1" Class 0-4-2 passenger tank locomotives were built between 1873 and 1887. Of these, Neilson built Nos. 233-267, the rest coming from the L.B.S.C.R. works at Brighton. The "D1"'s were designed for general working on London suburban and country branches and were powerful engines. "Stanford", illustrated, had a long life, being withdrawn in 1934 after 53 years of service. During the Marsh regime (1904-1911) the "D1" tanks were given up-to-date boilers with two rings; the name was on the second ring and Ramsbottom safety valves over the firebox.

GREAT EASTERN RAILWAY—1878.   The fifteen 2-6-0 goods engines built by Neilson for the G.E.R. were the first locomotives to appear on a British railway with the 2-6-0 or Mogul wheel arrangement. The leading wheels were carried in a Pony truck which Ahrons has aptly described as being "of somewhat complicated construction . . . impossible to describe clearly without drawings". The G.E.R. Moguls were bad steamers, heavy on coal and compared unfavourably with less powerful engines for heavy coal traffic. All had been scrapped within a decade.

LANCASHIRE & YORKSHIRE RAILWAY—1878.   The "Lanky" was an amalgam of a number of railways including the Manchester and Leeds and the Manchester and Bolton Lines, the Liverpool & Bury Railway, the Manchester, Bury & Rossendale Railway and the East Lancashire and West Lancashire railways. Barton Wright's design 4-4 side tank bogie passenger engines numbered 72 in all, of which ten were built by Neilson, including No.86 (illustrated). First to be scrapped after 22 years' service was the Neilson-built No.113 of 1879.

MIDLAND RAILWAY— 1881. No.1527 (illustrated) was one of a batch of 30 such 2-4-0 engines built by Neilson. S. W. Johnson was a user of the six-wheeled four-coupled type of engine and they were an M.R. favourite for many years. Similar engines with smaller coupled wheels, of the "No.1" Class, were taken off the fast expresses because of crank axle failures and these later types, with 6′ 9″ coupled wheels, replaced them, successfully hauling heavy trains at high speeds. A Neilson-built engine was at the Stephenson Centenary Exhibition of 1881. Cylinders were 18″ × 26″, working pressure 140 lb/sq. in. and weight in working order (less tender) 39 tons 10 cwt.

HIGHLAND RAILWAY—1885. The "Clyde Bogie" series of the 4-4-0 "Duke" Class all came from the [wor]ks of the short-lived Clyde Locomotive Company. "Bruce" was the first of the series and the first locomotive [to b]e built at the Clyde Co.'s works. No.76 went to the Edinburgh Exhibition of 1886, survived into the grouping [an]d was withdrawn from service in 1925.

[LO]NDON & SOUTH WESTERN RAILWAY—1883. W. Adams introduced these 4-4-2 bogie passenger tank [engi]nes, 11 out of a total of 71 being built by Neilson. On the first 12, built by Beyer Peacock, the tank capacity was [1,00]0 gallons but on the Neilson versions this was raised to 1,200 gallons. Cylinders were 17½″ × 24″, wheels 5′ 7″ [and] 3′ 0″ dia. and weight in working order 58 tons. A preserved example of this type of locomotive (Neilson works [No. 3]209, L.S.W.R. No.488) can be seen on the Bluebell Railway and is now repainted in L.S.W.R. livery.

TERFORD & LIMERICK RAILWAY (I) [5′ 3″]—1885. The first 25½-mile Limerick-Tipperary
on of the W.L.R. was opened in the autumn of 1848. The inside-cylinder 4-4-0 No.9
rryowen" (illustrated) was built by Dübs against a one-off order.

CALEDONIAN RAILWAY—1886. No.123 of the C.R. was designed and built by Neilson to the order of the
railway and was destined to be the only 4-2-2 to be used on a Scottish railway. In the race to the North of 1888 it
distinguished itself when, with a load of bogie coaches, it covered 103¾ miles (Carlisle-Edinburgh) in a daily
average time of 107¾ minutes. As the run included the ascent of Beattock Bank the performance of No.123 was
astonishing. Between 1930 and 1935 it worked Firth-Dundee trains and was the last "single" express engine to
operate in the U.K. It has one other claim to fame, having been built in 66 days from the receipt of order. No.123
can now be seen in the Glasgow Transport Museum.

RVAN & PORTPATRICK JUNCTION RAILWAY—1886. Of the 0-6-0 illustrated, two were built to the
gn of W. T. Wheatley who became General Manager of the G.P.J.R. in 1886. The line from Girvan made a
tion with the Portpatrick & Wigtownshire Junction Joint Railways at Challoch, from whence the G.P.J.R. had
ning powers over the Portpatrick Railway to Stranraer. The opening of the G.P.J.R. in 1887 provided the first
ct link between Glasgow and Stranraer. The two 0-6-0s, Nos.4 and 5, were withdrawn in 1914 and 1917
ectively.

GLASGOW & PAISLEY JOINT RAILWAY—1886.   Two small mineral tank engines, Nos. 1 and 2, were built by Neilson, of which No. 1 is illustrated. Cylinders were 14″ × 20″, wheels 3′ 8″ dia., fixed wheel base 7′ 0″, heating surface 685 sq. ft. and weight in working order 28 tons 14 cwt.

MANCHESTER, SHEFFIELD & LINCOLNSHIRE RAILWAY—1889.   An order for 35 of these 0-6-2 tank engines was executed by Neilson. Nicely proportioned, their cylinders were 18″ × 26″, wheels 5′ 1″ and 3′ 6″ dia., heating surface 1,278 sq. ft., tank capacity 1,300 gallons and weight in working order 61 tons. The fixed wheel base was long for the type—16′ 6″.

METROPOLITAN RAILWAY—1892.   Extensions of the M.R. from 1868 onwards necessitated more locomotives and Neilson built four Class "C" 0-4-4 tank engines, of which No.70 is illustrated. Cylinders were 18″ × 26″, wheels 5′ 6″ and 3′ 9⅛″ dia., and weight in working order 50 tons 8 cwt.

SOUTHWOLD RAILWAY [3′ 0″]—1893.   Nos.1 and 2 of the S.R. came from the Sharp, Stewart works. The railway opened in 1879 and closed in 1929. Average time for the Halesworth-Southwold journey of nine miles was 37 minutes. The S.R. remained derelict until 1941 when the rails were lifted, rolling stock dismantled and the locomotives cut up.

MIDLAND RAILWAY—1891. This graceful 4-4-0 bears the hall mark of t[...] Johnson locomotive outline and is, with some variations, of the same family as t[...] M.G.N.Jt.R. locomotive illustrated on this page. Cylinders were 18½″ × 26″, whe[...] 7′ 0″ and 3′ 6″ dia., working pressure 160 lb/sq. in. and weight in working order 44 to[...] 14 cwt. Sharp, Stewart built 20 of these engines, together with their 3,250 gall[...] capacity six-wheeled tenders.

MIDLAND & GREAT NORTHERN Jnt RAILWAY—1893. The M.G.N.Jt.R. was created in 1893 by the amalgamation of a number of smaller railways. There is again the Johnson touch about this "C" Class 4-4-0, ten of which were supplied by Sharp, Stewart. Cylinders were 18½″ × 26″, wheels 6′ 6″ and 3′ 3″ dia., working pressure 165 lb/sq. in. and weight in working order 39 tons 4 cwt. They closely resembled the Midland Railway "2203" Class save for slight variations in the smokebox. The six-wheeled tenders had a water capacity of 2,950 gallons and the lettering Jt.M.G.N.R. was changed at a later date.

BARRY RAILWAY—1894. The 0-4-4 bogie tank became a typically British product and these Sharp-built examples were representative. The type was a rarity outside the U.K. The "G" Class tanks of the B.R. were passenger engines (Nos.68 and 69 being built by Sharp, Stewart) and worked main passenger services all over the system. Cylinders were 18″ × 26″, wheels 5′ 7½″ and 3′ 0″ dia., working pressure 150 lb/sq. in. and weight in working order 54 tons 19 cwt.

GLASGOW & SOUTH WESTERN RAILWAY—1893. Ten of these 0-4-4 tanks were b
Neilson. While they have no outstanding features they are good examples of this once so popula
engine wheel arrangement which graced the metals of so many railways of the land. Cylinder
17¼″ × 24″, wheels 5′ 2″ and 3′ 1″ dia., tank capacity 1,000 gallons and weight in working order 5
11 cwt.

GREAT NORTH OF SCOTLAND RAILWAY—1893.   Neilson built nine 0-4-4 tanks such as the one illustrated, with 17½″ × 22″ cylinders. The illustrations of the Barry and Glasgow & South Western railways' 0-4-4 tanks (opposite and below) serve to show how great was the interest in this type of engine.

MIDLAND RAILWAY—1894.   This beautifully proportioned 0-4-4 tank locomotive was another of
Johnson's contributions to the M.R. stud and is an outstanding example of this peculiarly British type
of locomotive. Five of these engines were built by Dübs, No.2232 (illustrated) being the last of the

batch. Cylinders were 18″ × 24″, wheels 5′ 3½″ and 3′ 0½″ dia. This series of five was similar to another fifteen built by Dübs in 1894 and a previous twenty in 1892, with the one exception that Nos.2228–2232 were condensing engines.

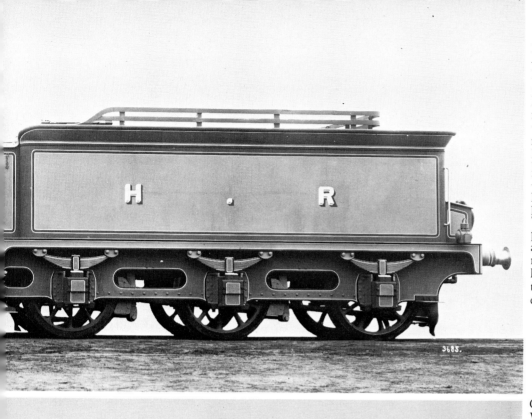

HIGHLAND RAILWAY —1897. When the "Small Ben" Class 4-4-0 No.1 (illustrated) left the works of Dübs in 1898 it bore the name "Ben Nevis" but within the same year it was renamed "Ben-y-Gloe". Designed by Peter Drummond, the "Small Bens" were not quite as powerful as their predecessors, the 4-4-0 "Loch" Class, but they were popular with the enginemen and earned a good reputation on the Inverness-Wick section of the H.R. where they were extensively employed.

GLASGOW & SOUTH WESTERN RAILWAY —1894. During his tenure of office James Manson gave to the "Sou'-West" a fine stud of locomotives, not the least of these being his 4-4-0s and their variants. No.344 was one of a batch of ten "336" Class 4-4-0 locomotives built by Dübs in 1895 but it differed from the others in that it was experimentally fitted with a water-tube type firebox which followed a design by Dugald Drummond. Their tractive effort was considerably higher than Manson's earlier "8" Class and they were capable of working with ease over the hilly sections of the G.S.W.R. in the Greenock and Stranraer areas of the line. The class numbered 25 engines in all.

DUKE OF SUTHERLAND'S RAILWAY—1895. This 0-4-4 tank, "Dunrobin", was built by Sharp, Stewart to work the Duke's private railway between Golspie and Helmsdale; the Duke and his heirs had the right to run it on the Highland Railway as they desired. It worked over the private line and the H.R. until 1920; it was last heard of as being preserved in running order near Vancouver, British Columbia.

GREAT NORTHERN RAILWAY—1897. This type of 0-6-0 shunting tank was developed by Ivatt from the Stirling design of 1874. Lined out and painted in G.N.R. livery they were good looking and nicely proportioned engines. Out of the 25 examples built by Sharp, Stewart against one order, G.N.R. No.1247 can be seen at Grosmont on the North Yorkshire Moors Railway.

CORK & BANDON RAILWAY (I) [5′ 3″]—1894.   The C.B.R. was completed, Cork to Bandon, in December 1851. Neilson supplied two broad-gauge 4-4-0 passenger tank engines, Nos.9 (illustrated) and 10. Cylinders were 16″ × 22″, coupled wheels 5′ 6″ dia. and weight in working order 41 tons 2 cwt.

TAFF VALE RAILWAY—1898.   Neilson built nine of these 0-6-2 tank locomotives for the T.V.R.—a railway which was originally built to 4′ 8½″ gauge, in spite of the fact that I. K. Brunel—the broad gauge advocate—was its engineer! Hurry Riches introduced this type of engine to the T.V.R. and its popularity spread throughout South Wales.

54   GREAT NORTHERN RAILWAY (I) [5′ 3″]—1898.   The 4-4-0 wheel arrangement was popular with the G.N.R.(I) and produced some good looking engines. "Apollo" was one of four built by Neilson. Coupled wheels were 6′ 7″ dia., cylinders 18½″ × 26″, working pressure 175 lb/sq. in. and weight in working order 46 tons.

HIGHLAND RAILWAY—1898.   Peter Drummond's 4-6-0 "Castle" Class became a fairly large series—a first series of 19, a second series of four and a third series of three. The Dübs-built engines were of the first series of 1900/1902 and totalled 10 engines. One of them, "Ballindalloch Castle", was equipped with a "Phoenix" superheater in 1912 but the results were unsatisfactory and it was soon removed. The "Castles" were designed as passenger engines; of the first series cylinders were 19½″ × 26″ and wheels 5′ 9″ and 3′ 3″ dia. They worked the heavy trains between Perth and Inverness with distinction. Comparative locomotive trials between the North British Railway and the H.R. involved "Skibo Castle"—another of the Dübs-built first series.

YMNEY RAILWAY—1899. The R.R., like so many of the other minor railways in South Wales,
a tank engine line. No.104, and the other nine locomotives of the same batch from Neilson's works,
presentative. A feature of R.R. tanks was the double frames, the outer ones taking the axles of the
led wheels. The popularity of the 0-6-2 tank locomotive on the railways of South Wales is
ated by the number taken over by the Great Western Railway at the time of grouping—446 all told.

NORTH BRITISH RAILWAY—1899. The N.B.R. had a good and varied selection of locomotives and the
0-6-0 tank illustrated has a pleasing appearance. A batch of 20 came from Sharp, Stewart, Nos.815-834. Cylinders
were 17″ × 26″, wheels 4′ 6″ dia., working pressure 150 lb/sq. in. and weight in working order 44 tons 19 cwt.

JEGAL RAILWAY (I) [3′ 0″]—1900. Narrow-gauge locomotives are almost always of interest
se of their distinctive design, and this 4-4-4 freight tank is no exception. Two were built by
on, No.10 "Sir James" being one of the pair. Cylinders were 14″ × 20″, wheels 4′ 0″ and 2′ 3″ dia.,
ing pressure 150 lb/sq. in., tank capacity 1,000 gallons and weight in working order 30 tons 10 cwt.
e couplers and buffers were fitted.

57

HIGHLAND RAILWAY—1901. The 0-6-0 "Barney" Class locomotives were designed by Peter Drummond and totalled 12 in all. Of these, six were built by Dübs in 1900, and a further four in 1902 (one example from the second batch is illustrated). Two more were built by N B L in 1907. The "Barneys" were designed for goods traffic and the first six were supplied with eight-wheeled tenders, but these were later replaced with six-wheeled ones similar to those supplied with the remainder of the class. The four engines built against the 1900 order (works Nos.4240-4243) were fitted with water tube fireboxes; cylinders were 18¼" × 26" and wheels 5′ 0″ dia. Nos.4241 and 4242 were withdrawn in 1946 and 1936 respectively, while Nos.4240 and 4243 were still in service in 1947.

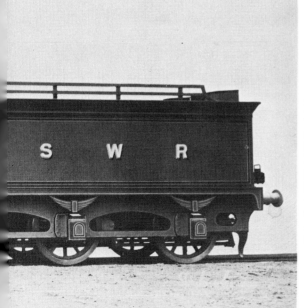

LONDON & SOUTH WESTERN RAILWAY—1900. Dübs was sufficiently proud of this 4-4-0 tender locomotive to exhibit it at the Glasgow International Exhibition of 1901. Apart from its looks, it had the unusual feature of a water-tube firebox following the Drummond system. The pleasing proportions of this locomotive are frequently commented upon and the attention paid to detail design is typical of the period. Although comparatively light (86 tons in working order) it was capable of fast running with heavy passenger trains. Like the 4-4-0s of the Midland Railway and the South Eastern & Chatham Railway, those of the L.S.W.R. possessed distinctive features which made them easily recognisable.

GREAT CENTRAL RAILWAY—1902. The 4-6-0 wheel arrangement grew rapidly in popularity after its introduction on the Highland Railway in the shape of the famous "Jones goods", built by Sharp, Stewart; the G.C.R. adopted the 4-6-0 wheel arrangement but, like other railways of that time, applied it to express passenger engines. Of the Robinson design illustrated, Neilson built a batch of six. Cylinders were 19″ × 26″, wheels 6′ 0″ and 3′ 6″ dia., working pressure 180 lb/sq. in., weight of locomotive in working order 65 tons 8 cwt. and tender 39 tons 6 cwt. The G.C.R. was the first railway in Britain to use the Belpaire firebox, which became a standard on the line.

GREAT CENTRAL RAILWAY—1902. The 0-8-0 wheel arrangement was popular for mineral engines and Robinson's version of it for the G.C.R. was both good looking and powerful. The wheel arrangement seemed to lend itself to good design and particularly where outside cylinders were employed. The Neilson-built series of three locomotives had cylinders 19″ × 26″, wheels 4′ 7″ dia., working pressure 180 lb/sq. in. and weight of locomotive and tender in working order 61 tons 5 cwt and 39 tons 6 cwt respectively.

61

LONDON, TILBURY & SOUTHEND RAILWAY—1902. The 4-4-2 express passenger tank engines with outside cylinders designed by T. Whitelegg and built by both Sharp, Stewart and Dübs represent this type of locomotive at its best, both in appearance and performance. All were named, "Mansion House" (illustrated) being a Dübs product. A tribute to the excellence of the design was the

Glasgow Loco: Works 15744.

building in 1907–1909 of a number of similar locomotives with enlarged cylinders 19″ × 26″. Details of the 1902 design were: cylinders 18″ × 26″, coupled wheels 6′ 6″ dia., working pressure 170 lb/sq. in. and weight in working order 63 tons 15 cwt. Water capacity was 1,500 gallons and coal 2 tons 5 cwt.

64

GREAT SOUTHERN & WESTERN RAILWAY (I) [5′ 3″]—1903. This illustration of an 0-6-2 tank locomotive marks the end of the Sharp Stewart, Neilson Reid and Dübs products and the beginning of the long series of locomotives produced by The North British Locomotive Co. Ltd. (NBL). It also indicates the very wide application of the 0-6-2 wheel arrangement to tank engines of all gauges.

SOUTH EASTERN & CHATHAM RAILWAY—1902. This 4-4-0, built by Dübs to the design of H. Wainwright, is yet another example of the popular 4-4-0, demonstrating its adaptability to design variations for differing power requirements. No.75 (illustrated) was one of a batch of ten "D" Class locomotives. Cylinders were 19″ × 26″ and coupled wheels 6′ 8″ dia.

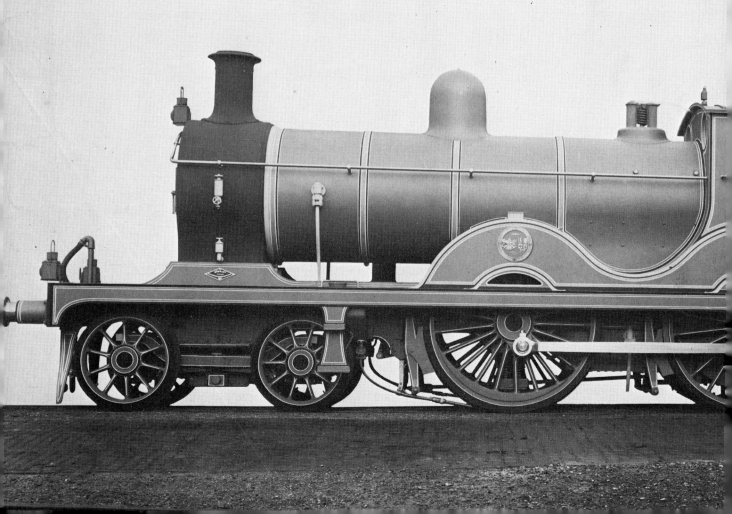

BARRY RAILWAY—1904. Railcars were never numerous in the order books of N B L but the two built for the B.R. are good examples, embodying the engineering of the power bogie, the craft of the coach builder and the skills of the paintshop. In the construction of the four-wheeled power bogie the coupled wheels were powered by two 12″ × 16″ cylinders, the valves being operated through Walschaerts valve gear. The vertical boiler was mounted on the bogie, with its centre immediately above the centre of rotation, while the central chimney appeared above the roof of the carriage body. All controls were mounted on the boiler itself. Heating surface was 598 sq. ft., working pressure 160 lb/sq. in. and weight of the bogie and boiler 18 tons 11½ cwt in working order. Water capacity (carried in a tank under the car body) was 500 gallons and coal capacity ¾ ton.

MIDLAND & SOUTH WESTERN JUNCTION RAILWAY—1905.

The M.S.W.J.R. was, like the Cambrian Railways, wedded to 0-4-4 engines for its passenger services, the first 4-4-0 coming from Dübs in 1893. The Class "L" No.1 (illustrated) was built by N B L against a one-off order and was followed by eight more between 1909 and 1914. Cylinders were 18″ × 26″, coupled wheels 5′ 0″ dia. and tractive effort 16,603 lbs. No.1 was withdrawn in 1935. When the Great Western Railway took over many small railways at the grouping, including the M.S.W.J.R and the Cambrian Railways, the 4-4-0s they inherited came from those two companies.

68

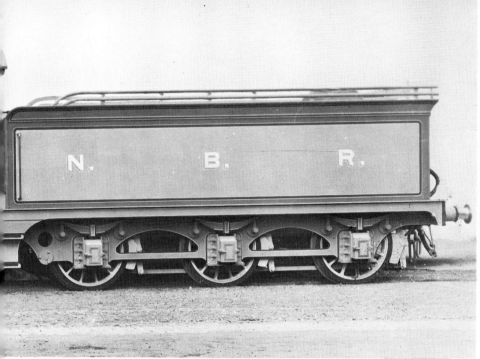

NORTH BRITISH
RAILWAY—1906. Of the
Atlantics of the N.B.R., N B L
built the first 14, No.868,
"Aberdonian", being the first of
the batch to be delivered. For
various reasons the early history
of these locomotives was not
impressive; they were dogged by
meddlers and much biased
comment. Superheating was
carried out during and after World
War I and the Atlantics eventually
proved their worth and were
acknowledged to be engines of
considerable merit.
"Aberdonian" was withdrawn in
1933—ten years after the N.B.R.
was absorbed by the London &
North Eastern Railway.

MARYPORT & CARLISLE RAILWAY—1907.
For the M.C.R. this 0-6-0 was essentially a goods
engine but was used for passenger work as well.
The chief merit of this type of locomotive was that
the entire weight in working order of 43 tons 10
cwt was available on the coupled wheels for adhe-
sion. Tractive force at 75% of boiler pressure was
15,410 lb. Cylinders were 18″ × 26″, wheels 5′ 1½″
dia. and working pressure 150 lb/sq. in. Tender
capacity was 2,500 gallons of water and fuel space
180 cu. ft.

GREAT CENTRAL RAILWAY—1905. The
G.C.R. Atlantics, designed by Robinson, were
generally acclaimed as being well proportioned
engines and are regarded as being typical of
outside-cylindered 4-4-2s of the period. Cylinders
were 19″ × 26″ and coupled wheels 6′ 9″ dia. It has
been said that N B L referred to the drawings of
these Atlantics, of which they had built 12, for
much of the design of the North British Railway's
Atlantics (illustrated on page 68) but this is incor-
rect and without justification. The G.C.R. Atlantics
were of Robinson design and were quite as individual as their N.B.R. counterparts and the two
earned individual reputations.

FURNESS RAILWAY—1906. Pettigrew's first 0-6-2 side tank locomotive, the "L1" Class, appeared in 1899, followed by the "L2" of 1904 and the "L3" (illustrated) of 1907. They were not superheated but proved themselves adaptable in service, from passenger train working to freight

L. 215.

traffic. The 24' wheelbase and trailing axle allowed for a rear bunker with a fuel capacity of 135 cu. ft. and a tank capacity of 1,700 gallons. Out of the weight in working order of 58 tons 11 cwt, 43 tons 17 cwt were on the coupled wheels. N B L built six of the Class "L3" engines against the one order.

NORTH EASTERN RAILWAY—1910. This 4-4-2 design of Wilson Worsdell's was one of the many interesting types which appeared during the great Atlantic era. It was an excellent example of a 3-cylinder engine, all cylinders being high pressure and all driving on the front axle—an arrangement which became standard on the N.E.R. Cylinders were 15½″ × 26″ and coupled wheels 6′ 10″ dia. N B L built ten of these engines against the first order and ten more against a second.

GLASGOW & SOUTH WESTERN RAILWAY—1912. The 4-4-0 "131" Class was the second of Peter Drummond's designs after his appointment as locomotive superintendent of the G.S.W.R. The six engines of the Class were all provided with Walschaerts valve gear, fitted inside and operated from an eccentric in lieu of the usual return crank. The engines were not superheated but, like the same designer's "279" Class 0-6-0s, they had steam-driers, feed pumps, steam reversers and tender heating equipment. The automatic vacuum brakes on engine and tender were supplemented (via train pipes), by a Westinghouse pump. Cylinders were 19½″ × 26″, wheels 6′ 0″ and 3′ 6″ dia., working pressure 180 lb/sq. in. and weights in working order 61 tons 17 cwt and 45 tons 5¼ cwt for engine and tender respectively.

FURNESS RAILWAY—1913. Of the Class "K4" 4-4-0 tender engines (No. 132 illustrated), N B L supplied two in 1913 and two in 1914. Designed by Pettigrew, costs were kept to a minimum by allowing N B L to use existing patterns. Cylinders were 18″ × 26″, coupled wheels 6′ 0″ dia. and working pressure 170 lb/sq. in. They were classed as main line engines and remained in service until after the grouping and the formation of the London, Midland & Scottish Railway, when the F.R. lost its identity.

TAFF VALE
RAILWAY—1914. It was left to
J. Cameron, who succeeded
Hurry Riches, to design the
largest and most powerful of the
T.V.R. 0-6-2 tank locomotives
and an order for six was placed
with N B L. These "A" Class
engines were ideal for the duties
demanded of them and they were
equally at home on mineral or
passenger services. Cylinders
were $18\frac{1}{2}'' \times 26''$, coupled wheels
5' 3" dia., working pressure 175
lb/sq. in. and weight in working
order 69 tons.

GLASGOW & SOUTH WESTERN RAILWAY—1910. In 1903 Manson's unsuperheated 4-6-0 "381" Class locomotives appeared. Ten had been ordered from Sharp, Stewart at the time of the amalgamation and were built by N B L. Good as his "381" design was, when Manson ordered two more in 1910, Nos. 128 (illustrated) and 129, they were both superheated and No. 129 was fitted with a Weir feedwater heater. They proved superior to the earlier engines of the class. Superheated, No. 128 showed an economy of 18¼% in coal and 21½% in water while No. 129, superheated and with feed-water heater, returned comparable figures of 26% and 22%. Both engines were capable of consistently good performances and 85 m.p.h. was frequently attained. The 91-mile Carlisle-Kilmarnock run was regularly timed at 101 minutes, including one stop.

NORTH BRITISH RAILWAY—1915.   The "M" Class 4-4-2 unsuperheated passenger tanks bu
between 1911 and 1913 were good engines but by 1915 more power was required to handle heavi
stock. To cope with this situation the Class "L" superheated 4-4-2 tank (illustrated) appeared,
coming from N B L; a further six came from the same works in 1920 to complete a class totalling
engines in all. Cylinders were 19″ × 26″, coupled wheels 5′ 9″ dia. and bogie and radial wheels 3′ 6″ an
3′ 9″ dia. respectively, working pressure 165 lb/sq. in., tractive force at 75% of boiler pressure 16,830
and weight in working order 73 tons 6 cwt.

HIGHLAND RAILWAY—1915.   The "Loch" locomotives built for the H.R. were three of a Class of 18 4-4-0
engines; They were the last of the series to be built and the last class of engines to be designed by Jones. Intended for
express passenger duties they were regarded as outstanding engines when first introduced in 1896. Although the
original photograph from which the illustration is taken is clearly marked with the N B L order No.L662, "Loch
Insh" was, in fact, the first locomotive of the Dübs-built batch of 1896!

L 667

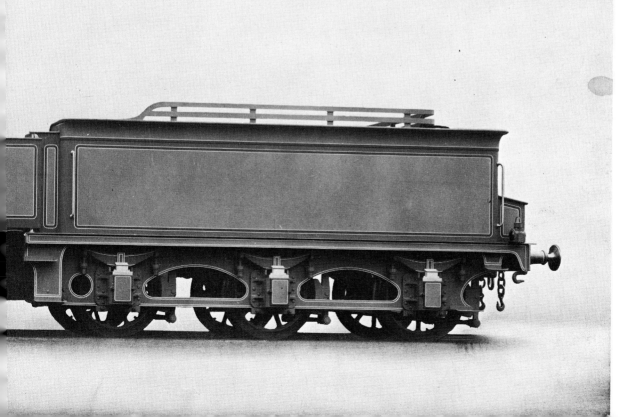

GLASGOW & SOUTH WESTERN RAILWAY—1916. Peter Drummond moved from the Highland to the G.S.W.R. in 1911 and designed the 0-6-0 tank engine illustrated for areas where sharp curves were prevalent. The wheels on the second axle were flangeless; the wheel base was only 10′ 0″ and the wheels 4′ 2″ dia. The 17″ × 22″ cylinders had Richardson balanced slide-valves with Walschaerts valve gear. Only three such engines were built.

84

LONDON & NORTH WESTERN RAILWAY—1915. Whale's "Experiment" Class of The Premier Line were good examples of the 4-6-0 locomotive and were followed by Bowen Cook's "Prince of Wales" Class 4-6-0 (illustrated), built between 1911 and 1921. N B L produced 20 of them. Joy valve gear was used but with some variations from that on the "Experiments". Overall, the "Princes" were better than the "Experiments", their performance being consistent and their hill climbing ability far better. Their success is emphasised by the number of engines in the class—245 in all. Cylinders were $20\frac{1}{2}'' \times 26''$, wheels 6′ 3″ and 3′ 9″ dia., working pressure 175 lb/sq. in. and tractive force at 75% of boiler pressure 19,120 lb.

GREAT NORTHERN RAILWAY—1920.   Gresley's Class "N2" 0-6-2 condensing tank locomotives were developed from Ivatt's Class "N1" tanks, one of which had been fitted with a Gresley twin-tube superheater and had proved its superiority. Of the many "N2"'s that were built, 50 came from N B L. Their squat appearance resulted from the loading gauge restrictions of the Metropolitan Railway's widened lines, over which the "N2" engines worked. No.1759 (illustrated) was about the fortieth of its type to come from N B L, the figure on the footplate being the late Duke of Windsor (then Prince of Wales) who was visiting the company's works to unveil the War Memorial window in the Administration building. Details of the locomotive are as follows: cylinders 19″ × 26″, wheels 5′ 8″ and 3′ 8″ dia., working pressure 170 lb/sq. in., tractive force at 75% of boiler pressure 17,590 lb and weight in working order 69 tons 14 cwt.

88 GREAT NORTHERN RAILWAY—1920. N B L built five of these Gresley-designed 2-8-0 three-cylinder locomotives—an adaptation of an earlier 2-8-0 mineral engine. The main differences were the employment of three cylinders (as opposed to the two of the originals) and the lowering of the outside cylinders to an almost horizontal position. Valve gear included two sets outside and derived gear for the third (inside) cylinder. Other lessons learned from Gresley's first three-cylinder locomotive (No.461

2-8-0 of 1918) were the enlargement of the cylinders (18″ to 18½″ dia.) and an increase in boiler pressure (170 to 180 lb/sq. in.). The inside cylinder was very steeply inclined to bring the steam chests into line. The excellence of the engines is emphasised by their adoption as the standard heavy freight engine of the London & North Eastern Railway.

HIGHLAND RAILWAY—1908.   The 4-4-0 "Big Ben" Class locomotive illustratd
was one of two designed and ordered from N B L by Drummond. Like the 0-6-4
banking tank engines they were not superheated, as Drummond did not favour its use.
"Ben Bhreag Mhor" (illustrated) and "Ben a'Chaoruinn" (Nos.60 and 62 respectively) were the last two of the Class to be built and were supplied with eight-wheel
tenders. No.60 was withdrawn in 1932 and No.62 in 1937. The "Big Ben" Class
totalled six engines in all.

90

HIGHLAND RAILWAY—1908. The 0-6-4 "No.39" Class banking tank engine (illustrated) was designed by Peter Drummond and was the last class to be introduced to the H.R. by him. Of the total of eight "No.39"'s, all were built by N B L between 1909 and 1912. No.39, the first to be built, outlasted all the others, being withdrawn in 1936. Cylinders were $18\frac{1}{4}'' \times 26''$ and coupled wheels 5' 0" dia.

GLASGOW & SOUTH WESTERN
RAILWAY—1920. Whitelegg was, as
an ex-London, Tilbury & Southend
Railway man, a natural protagonist of
the main line tank engine. Just before
leaving the L.T.S.R. he designed a 4-6-4
Baltic tank and six were built. They
were the subject of much discussion.
When Whitelegg joined the G.S.W.R.
the 4-6-4 engine still intrigued him and
in 1920 he produced his design for a
Baltic tank engine and six were built by
N B L. They were the first engines of
this type to be used in Scotland and, like
the 4-6-4 Baltics of the L.T.S.R.,
became a source of discussion and
argument. Externally they were superb
looking engines but it is questionable
whether they were right for the
G.S.W.R. Cylinders were 22″ × 26″,
wheels 6′ 0″ and 3′ 6″ dia., working
pressure 160 lb/sq. in., tractive force at
75% of boiler pressure 23,590 lb and
weight in working order 99 tons 1 cwt.
Fuel space was 159 cu. ft. and tank
capacity 2,400 gallons.

CALEDONIAN RAILWAY—1922.

Pickersgill's last 4-6-0 design was for a non-superheated engine for the Oban line. Only eight were built, all by N B L. These "Oban" engines had outside cylinders 19½″ × 26″, wheels 5′ 6″ and 3′ 6″ dia., working pressure 185 lb/sq. in., tractive force at 75% of boiler pressure 20,780 lb and weight in working order (minus tender) 62 tons 15 cwt. They were the last C.R. engines to be built before the railway grouping of 1923. Of nice appearance in their livery of "Caley" blue, they were, nevertheless, disappointing in service and were no better than McIntosh's "Oban" Class 4-6-0s of 1902-1905.

LONDON & NORTH EASTERN RAILWAY—1923.

Nigel Gresley's original "A1" Class Pacific proved itself to be a well designed engine and in 1923 the construction of another 40 was embarked upon—20 from Doncaster and 20 from N B L. No.2563 emerged from the Glasgow works with the unusual name of "William Whitelaw", whereas the other 19 were named after race horses. The three-cylinder "A1"'s were a milestone in locomotive history and the L.N.E.R. proudly exhibited No.4472, "Flying Scotsman", at the British Empire Exhibition at Wembley in 1924. This brought an automatic response from the Great Western Railway, whose 4-6-0 No.4073, "Caerphilly Castle", appeared on a stand alongside. The famous exchanges of 1925 saw the G.W.R. No.4079, "Pendennis Castle", competing with L.N.E.R. "Flying Fox". The result was the adoption by the L.N.E.R. of long travel valves—a feature of the success of G.W.R. front-end design.

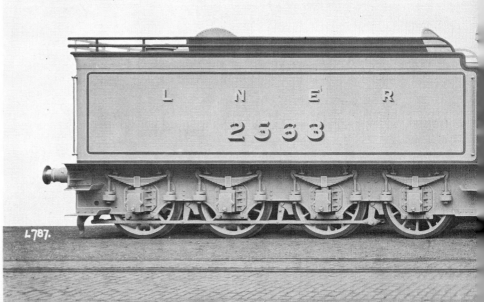

UTHERN RAILWAY—1924. The 4-6-0 "King Arthur" Class locomotives of the S.R. were
ect descendants of Urie's "N15" 4-6-0s of 1918. The 30 built by N B L, including "Sir Valence"
ustrated), were generally referred to as the "Scotch Arthurs". These successful engines embodied
g-lap, long-travel valves which then became standard practice on the Southern. In the development
the "N15" the valve gear was the most important feature, but improved smokebox draughting,
uced cylinder diameter and increased boiler pressure were contributory factors.

SOUTHERN RAILWAY—1925. The "L1" Class 4-4-0 locomotives of the Southern were successful from the
start of their career, the first 15 being built by N B L. They were modified versions of an earlier "L" Class 4-4-0 of
1914. The Maunsell "L1" had increased valve travel, modified chimney and smokebox arrangement and rede-
signed cab layout. N B L built Nos.753 to 759 (illustrated) and 782 to 789. The Class as a whole gave remarkably
good and consistent results in service as passenger engines. Dimensions and weights were: cylinders $19\frac{1}{2}'' \times 26''$;
wheels 6' 8" and 3' 7" dia.; working pressure 180 lb/sq. in., tractive force at 75% of boiler pressure 16,680 lb and
weight in working order (engine only) 58 tons 2 cwt.

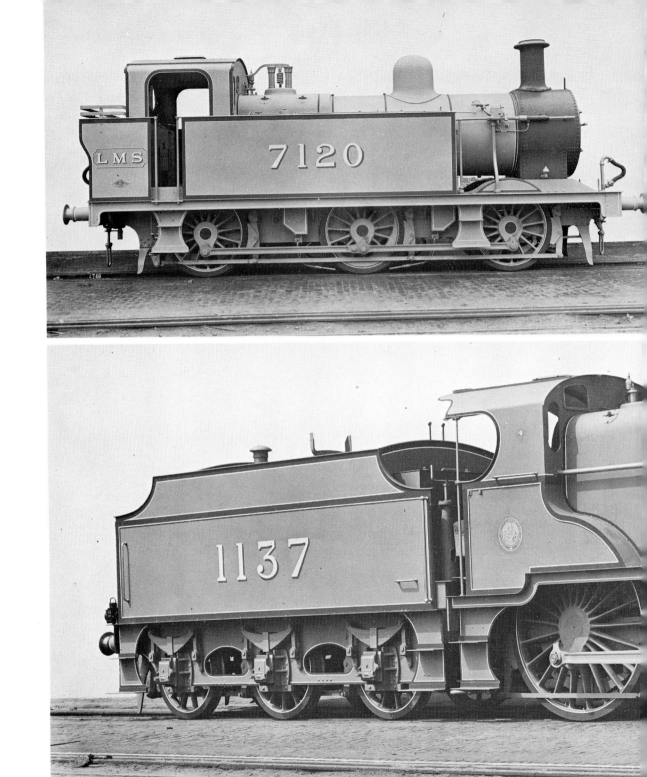

NDON, MIDLAND & SCOTTISH RAILWAY—1923.   The "7100" Class 0-6-0 shunting tank
omotive dates back to a Johnson design of 1899 for the Midland Railway and as rebuilt by Fowler.
iginally known as Class "3" and later as "3F", they numbered several hundreds and came from the
rks of various builders. Nos.7120 (illustrated) to 7134 and 16400-16459 were built by N B L.
n-superheated, the "7100"'s were rugged, simple and comparatively easy to maintain; they could be
n shunting, banking, handling local freight, etc., and, like so many of the railway's "maids of all
rk", continued their duties unloved and unsung.

LONDON, MIDLAND & SCOTTISH RAILWAY—1924.   S. W. Johnson's 4-4-0 compounds of 1901-1903,
built on the Smith system, set an example on the Midland Railway which was perpetuated by Deeley and
continued by Sir Henry Fowler of the L.M.S.R. In 1924 forty more 4-4-0 compounds were built at Derby and, out
of a further 100, 25 came from N B L. This spate of building was prompted by the success of Deeley's M.R.
compounds—considered to be the best of their type in the U.K. They could be worked as simple, semi-compound
and compound—the last mentioned when running, when all the h.p. exhaust went to the two outside l.p. cylinders.
For starting, steam at full pressure entered the h.p. steam chest and the l.p. chests via a reducing valve, the engine
thus working as a simple. For maximum power the engine could be worked as a semi-compound. Those built by
N B L had cylinders 19″ dia. (h.p.) and 21″ dia. (l.p.) × 26″ stroke, wheels 6′ 9″ and 3′ 6½″ dia., working pressure 200
lb/sq. in., tractive force at 60% of boiler pressure 20,857 lb and weight in working order (minus tender) 63 tons 10
cwt.

LONDON, MIDLAND & SCOTTISH RAILWAY—1926. In 1926 the Great Western Railway loaned one of its "Castle" Class engines to work over L.M.S.R. metals. The results of the trials served only to demonstrate its complete superiority and it was decided that a three-cylinder 4-6-0 was necessary for the L.M.S.R. if the new Anglo-Scottish services planned for 1927 were to be an unqualified success. N B L was given an order early in 1927 for 50 new 4-6-0s straight off the drawing board, there being no time for trials or possible modifications. The building of the engines was split between the Hyde Park and Queens Park works and the first to be completed left the latter works on July 14, 1927; it was No.6100, named "Royal Scot". By November of the same year the entire order had

been completed. This industrial *tour de force* enabled the L.M.S.R. to inaugurate its "Royal Scot" train in September 1927, running non-stop between Euston and Carlisle. These now famous 4-6-0s gave the L.M.S. what it wanted—a really powerful and fast express locomotive and one capable of handling with ease trains of 420 tons. The 18″ × 26″ inside cylinder drove the leading axle and the two outside cylinders the second one. Rebuilding of the Class began in 1943 and the rebuilt "Royal Scots" became one of the most powerful 4-6-0 types in the U.K. and for fast running they earned an enviable reputation.

GREAT WESTERN RAILWAY—1928.   When C. B. Collett had taken over as C.M.E. of the G.W.R. considerable new design work was started, ranging from "Castles" to 0-6-0 pannier tank locomotives. A new design for an 0-6-0 was developed from the rebuilt "2721" Class and N B L received an order for the first 50 of the new "5700" Class 0-6-0 pannier tank engines. Their construction continued for about 20 years and they constituted the largest of all classes on the G.W.R. Non-superheated, they had 17½″ × 24″ cylinders, 4′ 7½″ dia. wheels, a working pressure of 200 lb/sq. in., heating surface 1,178 sq. ft., a tractive effort of 19,860 lb and weight in working order 51 tons 13 cwt. The "5700"s replaced all the pannier tanks with 4′ 7½″ wheels as designed by Armstrong & Dean. The series built by N B L were Nos.5700 (illustrated) to 5749 and deliveries were effected weekly, the entire order being executed between December 1928 and April 1929. The "5700"s were typical of G.W.R. individuality.

LONDON, MIDLAND & SCOTTISH RAILWAY—1935. After the introduction of the "4" Class two-cylinder 2-6-4 tank locomotives, eight of which were built at Derby, various batch appeared including 75 from N B L and of which No.2561 (illustrated) was the first to be completed. T 19⅝" × 26" cylinders, with outside Walschaerts gear, were steamed by a boiler with a total heati surface of 1,450 sq. ft. (including superheater) and at 85% of boiler pressure (200 lb/sq. in.) produce tractive force of 24,670 lb. They were equipped with water pick-up gear for use when running in eith direction.

LONDON, MIDLAND & SCOTTISH RAILWAY—1933. A batch of 50 4-6-0 locomotives, the "5XP" Class (illustrated) which were later to be known as the "Jubilees", was ordered from N B L. They were to join another 191 engines which made up the Class and were numbered 5552 to 5742. It was in 1935 that one engine was named "Silver Jubilee" to commemorate the Silver Jubilee of King George V and from that time the "5XP"'s became better known as the "Jubilees". Nos.5735 and 5736 (named "Comet" and "Phoenix" respectively and both from N B L) were rebuilt and given enlarged boilers, double chimneys and blastpipes, and boiler pressure put up from 225 to 250 lb/sq. in. Tractive effort rose from 23,480 to 29,590 lb.

LONDON & NORTH EASTERN RAILWAY—1928. Of the 4-6-0 "Sandringhams", or "B17" Class engines, the first 10 were built by N B L. The increased weight of these three-cylinder engines (76 tons 13 cwt) was acceptable because of the better balancing and reduced hammer-blow inherent in the three-cylinder locomotive. Drive was divided—inside cylinder on the leading axle and outside cylinders on the axle of the middle pair of coupled wheels. "Sandringham" (illustrated) and others of the Class were popular with footplatemen and No.2800 made some notably fast runs over the Great Eastern section of the L.N.E.R. The "B17"'s in general earned for themselves a name for liveliness.

LONDON & NORTH EASTERN RAILWAY—1935.   The three-cylinder Class "K3" 2-6-0 or Mogul locomotives of the L.N.E.R. were extremely versatile mixed traffic engines. No.2467 (illustrated) was one of a batch of 20 built by N B L. They could make a good showing with a load of 650 tons and on passenger services speeds of 75 m.p.h. were common. Engine men always referred to them as being "lively". Being a three-cylinder simple all cylinders were $18\frac{1}{2}'' \times 26''$; wheels were 5' 8" and 3' 2" dia., working pressure 180 lb/sq. in., tractive force at 85% of boiler pressure 30,030 lb and weight in working order (engine only) 73 tons 2 cwt.

LONDON & NORTH EASTERN RAILWAY—1945. Of the Thompson type of "B1" Class locomotives N B L built one batch of 100, of which No. 1040, "Roedeer" (illustrated), is a fair example. Because of stringent war economies the designer made use of standard parts such as coupled wheels of the "V2", cylinders of the ex-G.N. "K2" and boiler of the "B17". Using components of proven efficiency made the "B1"'s useful engines, while their simplicity ensured ease of maintenance. Their

appearance and finish were a tonic to railwaymen and the public who had grown very tired of war time gloom and austerity which had become so apparent in details of external design, finish and maintenance. Some details of the N B L batch of "B1"'s are as follows: cylinders 20″ × 26″, wheels 6′ 2″ and 3′ 2″ dia., working pressure 225 lb/sq. in., total heating surface 2,005 sq. ft., tractive force at 85% of boiler pressure 27,000 lb and weight in working order (excluding tender) 71 tons 6 cwt.

110 BRITISH RAILWAYS—1948. Of Thompson's standard two-cylinder types for the L.N.E.R., his Class "K1" was a rebuild from a Gresley three-cylinder "K4" 2-6-0. The B.R. "K1" Moguls followed the Thompson rebuild very closely but there were differences in the weights in working order of both engine and tender; in Thompson's standard type "K1"s they were 66.85 tons and 44.20 tons respectively, whereas the N B L counterparts were 65.85 tons and 51.70 tons. The success of Gresley's Moguls goes right back to 1914 and it is not surprising that the B.R. "K1"s followed Thompson's "K4" rebuild. The cylinder dimensions of 20″ × 26″ were the same for Thompson's other standard types—the "01" 2-8-0 and the "K4" 2-6-0.

BRITISH RAILWAYS—1948. As far as this pictorial record of N B L is concerned this 2-6-4 "L1" Class locomotive marks the demise of the "Big Four" and the beginning of the railways of Britain under nationalisation. In 1945 Thompson of the L.N.E.R. produced his Class "L1" standard 2-6-4 tank engine and the 35 built for B.R. by N B L (No.67731 illustrated) were replicas. Cylinders were 20″ × 26″, wheels 5′ 2″ and 3′ 2″ dia., working pressure 225 lb/sq. in., total heating surface 1,620 sq. ft., tractive force at 85% of boiler pressure 32,080 lb and weight in working order 90 tons 17 cwt. Tank capacity was 2,630 gallons. Weight on the coupled wheels was 58 tons 4 cwt. A glance at the "L1" illustrated will show that it is, in fact, a tank engine version of the "K1", the rear bogie carrying the bunker and its maximum load of 4½ tons of fuel.

STEAM IN ACTION
BR
DIESE
IN ACTIO
GREAT WESTERN
STEAM DOUBLEHEADED
SCOTTISH
STEAM
IN THE 1920s
STEAM LOCOMOTI
LNERSTEA
SPECIALS
GREAT WESTERN
STEAM ON SHED
INDUSTRIAL
NARROW
GAUGE
RAILWAYS
IN BRITAIN
in action
NORTH EAS
STEAM
MORE
SOUTHER
SOUTHER
STEAM FROM LI
DIESELS
BR STANDARD
BRITANNIA PACIFICS
INDUSTRIAL
STEAM
IN ACTION
LONDON MIDLAND
STEAM
MIDLAND
GREAT WESTERN
STEAM IN ACTION 2
SOUTHER
STEAM
SKIPTON-CARLISLE
MORE BRITISH
NARROW GAUG
STEAM
LMSR
STEAM
H.C. CASSERLEY
OUTH AND EAST
REAT WESTERN
STEAM IN CLOSE-UP
AUSTRIAN STEAM
ELECTRIC
LOCOMOTIVES
OF THE WORLD
SCOTTISH
TH EAST
MEMORIES OF
STEAM
AROUND BRITAIN
STEAM